Ian and the Gigantic Leafy Obstacle

Sheila Miller

Illustrations by Meg Riddell

OMF BOOKS

Published by Overseas Missionary Fellowship (IHQ) Ltd.
2 Cluny Road, Singapore 259570, Republic of Singapore

First published *1983*
Reprints *1984, 1991, 1997, 2003*
This printing *2008*

OMF Books are distributed by
OMF, 10 West Dry Creek Circle, Littleton, CO 80120, USA
OMF, Station Approach, Borough Green, Sevenoaks, Kent TN15 8BG, UK
OMF, PO Box 849, Epping, NSW 2121, Australia
OMF, 5155 Spectrum Way, Bldg. 21, Mississauga, ON L4W 5A1, Canada
OMF, PO Box 10159, Auckland, New Zealand
and other OMF offices.

ISBN 9971-83-790-0

Part 1

"No doubt about it — I'm stuck!" said Ian, rubbing his head ruefully. "I can't get down the mountain again."

"We couldn't shift that great fellow with our small saws," one Thai man commented. The whole group gathered round him in the sunshine thought the same.

"It's absolutely gi-*nor*mous!"

"I can't even see over the top of it."

"Whatever caused it to fall down?"

"Wow! What a *big* tree!"

"Yes," agreed Ian, "it's a big tree."

The stronger men poked at it. Then they tried pushing its massive trunk. Its great jungly head rustled but it stayed where

it was, like a huge leafy giant who had fallen asleep right across his bed and refused to roll over.

The sun shone hot, as it always does in Thailand. Its burning beams beat down on the group of villagers and on the tall missionary from Scotland who had driven right up the mountain to their village-at-the-end-of-the-road.

They stared at the tree. A hum of conversation, like the whirring of the cicadas, interrupted the mountain stillness. Everyone was trying to think of an idea for moving the leafy giant.

"Teacher! Teacher! I know!" suddenly a young nut-brown man called out. "You told us that God answers prayer. Well, why don't you pray now? Ask God to move the tree!"

Silence fell on the colourful group. Yes, that was it! The white man had come up their mountain in his landrover, to tell them about God. He'd spent two days in their village, far away from the noisy cities. He'd brought a thing called a projector which had a light like a little moon shining in the dusky

tropical night. And it made pictures. The pictures had been about a man called Jesus, the Son of God.

"He can forgive all our wrong things," the missionary had told them, "and you won't need to be afraid of evil spirits any more. Jesus can make life worthwhile. He can take us to His beautiful home in heaven when we die." And yes, he had said that his God could answer prayer.

Ian swallowed nervously. Yes, yes, of course he believed God answered prayer, but — a *tree*? Could it really suddenly disappear from the mountain track?

And then he remembered something quite remarkable. It was a verse in the Bible and, strange to say, it was about a tree. Jesus had said, "If you have faith you could say to this tree, 'Pull yourself up by the roots and plant yourself in the sea', and it would obey you."

"Incredible!" thought Ian. "I've never seen a tree move in answer to prayer — but there's always a first time!"

So right there, in front of all the village people, he said in the Thai language, "Dear Father-God, I've told these folk about you. Now I need to get down to the next village to tell the people there. Please move the tree off the track so I can get through. Amen."

Ian opened his eyes. Could the tree possibly be gone? He was almost afraid to look. He raised his head. And... the tree was there — still there, big, leafy, tangled as ever, blocking his way down the road.

But someone else was there too — a stranger, running towards them.

"Teacher! Teacher!" called the stranger. "Don't go away!"

"That's easy," thought Ian, chuckling. "I can't!"

"Teacher, will you come and show the films up in *our* village?"

"I've just spent two days in your village," replied Ian, puzzled.

"No, no!" explained everybody, talking at once. "He's not from *this* village. He's from the *next* village."

Ian was bewildered. After all, had he not driven up the mountain

as far as anyone could go? He had decided to start his teaching tour at the village-at-the-end-of-the-road and then work down the track back home, stopping at all the other villages on the way. Then if the monsoon rains came early he'd not be caught out with his landrover and equipment too far away.

"I didn't know there was a next village," he said.

But there was. The village-at-the-end-of-the-road wasn't really the village-at-the-end-of-the-road after all!

The thing was, how to get there? No road! Not even a path!

"I can't show the films unless I can bring the landrover," he explained, "and there isn't a road."

9

"Oh yes, there's a road all right," the stranger assured him. "You can bring it easily."

Ian climbed into the landrover and revved the engine. He leaned hard on the gear stick, reversed, wrenched the steering wheel round and set off with the stranger to the real village-at-the-end-of-the-road.

The little crowd who had come out to help and offer advice ran along behind, some catching up with the landrover and perching on top of it until it looked like an enormous coloured ball of bees inching its way along the track. When they reached the village the extra passengers jumped off and waved goodbye to the landrover as it searched for a road leading further up the mountain.

"Through this paddy-field," instructed Ian's guide. Across the next and the next they manoeuvred, getting stuck once or twice on the little bridges between fields. After that the landrover nosed its way along a little jungle track which petered out

eventually by a stream.

"Now where's the road gone?" asked Ian.

"That's the road," pointed the stranger.

"That's not a road! It's a stream," Ian reasoned.

"It's a road too!" his guide explained.

Up, up the stream they drove, and when the boulders on its bed barred their way they jumped out into the water and heaved them off to the side. Two hours and a mile and a half later the stream brought them out in the centre of the real village-at-the-end-of-the-road.

Part 2

Mr Boon was worried. Six miles away over the hill he sat on the outskirts of a logging camp and thought. Then he thought some more and was worried all over again.

The afternoon sun shone hot, and if he hadn't been so anxious he might have fallen asleep right where he was, because he was an old man now and bent over and tired.

But this was no time for sleep. Instead he struggled to his feet, grabbed his little wooden stick and went across to check the grazing ground just once more.

"Tusker!" he cried. "Tus-ker-r-r!" But Tusker didn't come. His other four elephants were still grazing happily. Only Tusker was missing. His favourite.

He hobbled off to where the Thai men were packing up the camp.

"It's no good," he told them. "I'll have to go and look for him."

An elephant was too valuable a possession to lose.

"Take some food," one of the Thai men advised. "You might not find him for hours."

"And take the chains," another suggested, "to keep him with you when you catch him."

"Be careful," they warned. "The jungle is full of wild animals."

Sadly Mr Boon set off. "Perhaps I shall never see Tusker again," he thought. "Perhaps he's been stolen. Yes! That'll be it," he decided, for he noticed that Tusker's tracks led ahead in a straight line as though he were being led.

Night time comes quickly in Thailand. Soon the afternoon sun had disappeared behind the jungle trees. The shadows were long; the forest eerie. Mr Boon knew it was dangerous to go on. It was now so dark that he couldn't see Tusker's tracks any longer nor keep a look-out for snakes in the undergrowth.

Although bent and old, Mr Boon was used to life in the rough. With the help of a swinging vine he managed to climb a low tree and there, cradled in its branches, he wearily ate his supper and soon fell fast asleep.

It wasn't until the dark sky in the east was lightening to silver-grey that Mr Boon woke up. The jungle birds were quite delighted that dawn was breaking. They welcomed it with long hoots and screeches so that Mr Boon couldn't sleep any longer.

"Tusker!" he thought. "I must find him. It's light enough to follow his tracks again." He slid down the tree, clutching the remainder of his supper, the chains for trapping the elephant

and his little old stick.

All day long he followed Tusker's tracks. He could see where his elephant had stopped to eat and when satisfied had plodded on — still going straight ahead. "He can't have been stung by bees, then," thought Mr Boon. "And he certainly isn't on the rampage. These tracks show that he isn't even running. How strange!"

The only answer seemed to be that indeed someone *had* taken Tusker and was leading him away. Mr Boon wished the tell-tale hoof prints would come to an end with a big bulky elephant standing still in the jungle. But though he tracked him all that day, darkness came again with Tusker still missing. And once more the little old man climbed a tree to spend the night — this time without any supper to eat.

A hornbill screeched. Morning was again waking the jungle world, holding out a promise like a bright rainbow that perhaps today... today Mr Boon would find Tusker.

And yes! There he was! Big, bulky, beautiful — his grey skin baggy and wrinkly as if it were too big for him! Nobody with him either. No thief to tackle.

"Tusker!" grunted Mr Boon in delight, pulling out his chains. But as he bent his head, the big unwieldy creature started off again! He just wouldn't stay still long enough to be caught... as though his journey hadn't yet ended.

Part 3

"Is that tree down the road still there?" asked Ian. Two days had gone by since he'd left the first village to lurch over paddy-fields and stream to the real village-at-the-end-of-the-road. Again his projector had been shining in the velvety shadows of the night.

The headman emerged from his wooden house. The tree — still there? "I don't know — I suppose so," he said. "It was yesterday, and no trucks have been through the village. I'll come with you and have a look."

Of course the whole village wanted to see too and out trooped the colourful throng all over again.

"The people in the top village were so glad to hear about

Jesus," Ian told them. "In fact, I feel that God allowed the tree to fall across the road so that I could go up there and tell them!"

"Teacher!" called the young man who'd spoken out before. "I want to tell you something. There aren't any more villages so you'd better pray again. Perhaps this time your God will move the tree."

The landrover came grinding to a halt. They'd reached the point where the road led down the mountain.

Yes. The tree was still there.

Everyone spilled on to the track and again, in the Thai language so they all could understand, Ian prayed:

"Thank you, Lord, for guiding me to that other village. But now I need to get home before the rainy season starts. You know we can't move this tree, so please will you move it for us? Amen."

Slowly, carefully, Ian opened his eyes. The air was still. Only the jungle birds called to one another and in some distant tree gibbons whooped. The Thai people watched breathlessly.

The tree was still there.

But a little man had appeared. He was standing peering up at the missionary as though he'd never seen a foreigner before. With his bent back and little wooden stick, he looked as though he'd just stepped out of a nursery rhyme book right where the words say, "There was a crooked man who walked a crooked mile..."

"Where's he from?" asked the crooked little man, pointing at Ian, "and where's he going?"

"I came from down the mountain," answered Ian for himself, surprising the newcomer by speaking in Thai, "and I plan to go to some villages down the road."

"You can't. There's a tree in the way," stated the little old man.

"That's right. We're wondering about the best way of moving it," explained Ian patiently.

The bent-over little man shuffled across and poked the tree with his little walking stick. Then he prodded at the branches. He walked round it — poking and prodding; prodding and poking.

"I'll move the tree," he said. And with this strange promise he trudged off down the road on the other side.

❖   ❖   ❖

Standing on tip-toe to look over the massive trunk, Ian watched the crooked little man disappear into the jungle.

"He's crazy!" exclaimed the villagers. "How can an old man like that move such a big tree? Haven't *we* tried — all together — and couldn't?"

"Where did he come from?" Ian asked.

"We've never seen him before," they told him. "Crazy, that's what he is, turning up so mysteriously, calmly saying he'll move the tree and then disappearing into the jungle again!" And they began to laugh.

But quite suddenly the tittering faded away. What was that? That rustling noise, that crackling in the jungly undergrowth?

Nearer, steadily nearer it came, like a ghostly shiver among the trees, drowning out the merriment of the villagers.

Craning their necks, they stared down the track. The shuffling was somehow disturbing branches, making dry leaves crunch. Nearer it came. Nearer...

Even the hot morning air seemed to shimmer in surprise as it happened — into view came the little crooked man. High... high above the fallen tree. Riding a big, wrinkled grey elephant!

"That's right, Tusker," he hollered. "Trunk round it! You move it! Good old Tusker! That's a fine fellow!"

The elephant felt for the shape of the giant

leafy obstacle with his sensitive trunk. Curling it round the mighty tree, the great bulky creature heaved and pushed. Then it heaved some more while the little old man kept yelling encouragement from the top of its neck.

The villagers stood by in amazement, watching till Tusker had propelled the tree far enough off the track to leave room for Ian to edge the landrover round it.

"There you are," said the little old man, sliding down off the elephant. "I've moved the tree."

"Little old man, where have you come from?"

"How did you manage to be here just at the right moment?"

The Thai people shelled him with questions.

"I'm from the logging camp, six miles away over the hill," answered their helper. "I own five elephants."

"Oh-ooh," said everybody. "Five elephants! He's a very wealthy man!"

"Two days ago," he continued, "I put my elephants out to

graze. This one here, my favourite old Tusker, wandered straight off into the jungle. He often does that, you know, but he comes back in the afternoon."

He paused, looking at the crowd. Then he said, "This time he didn't come back."

And Mr Boon told the throng of quiet villagers all about his adventures in the jungle, tracking down old Tusker.

"Just down the road there, I caught up with him once again," finished old Mr Boon. "I slid the chains on as fast as I could before he escaped another time and then... well, then I heard voices — your voices. I came out of the jungle to ask for some food before I start off home."

Ian stood there, drinking in every word. His astonishment began to change to happiness. He felt like dancing and he wanted to shout and sing!

Two days ago he had stood right here on this spot and had

asked God to move the tree and, just two days ago, Tusker had strayed. God had begun answering the very moment he had prayed.

Ian leaped into the landrover, waving and calling goodbye to his Thai friends. He steered it towards the now-clear space on the mountain track, his thoughts tumbling over each other.

"While the elephant was on its way to move the tree, God sent me to that other village," he mused, "the one I didn't even know was there, the real village-at-the-end-of-the-road. The obstacle in the track meant I could tell other people about Jesus.

"I'm glad it all happened," he decided. "I was right. God *does* answer prayer and now I know He can even turn a difficulty into a launching pad for one of His special miracles.

"Wow! Wait till I tell them this story when I get home. It's like something out of a book..."

Pressing his foot down hard on the accelerator, Ian sent his dauntless little landrover hurtling down the hill towards village-number-three-from-the-end-of-the-road.